D0883067

54,427

8/77

A Bear, a Bobcat and Three Ghosts

Anne Rockwell

Ready-to-Read

MACMILLAN PUBLISHING CO., INC.
NEW YORK

Copyright © 1977 Anne Rockwell

All rights reserved. No part of this book may be reproduced or transmitted in any form or by any means, electronic or mechanical, including photocopying, recording or by any information storage and retrieval system, without permission in writing from the Publisher.

Macmillan Publishing Co., Inc.
866 Third Avenue, New York, N.Y. 10022
Collier Macmillan Canada, Ltd.

Printed in the United States of America

10   9   8   7   6   5   4   3   2   1

LIBRARY OF CONGRESS CATALOGING IN PUBLICATION DATA

Rockwell, Anne F
  A bear, a bobcat, and three ghosts.

  (Ready-to-read)
  SUMMARY: The traveling peddler Timothy Todd and his friends become involved in a moonlight chase with a bear, a bobcat, and three ghosts.
    [1. Humorous stories.   2. Halloween—Fiction]
I. Title.
PZ7.R5943Be   [E]   77-5084
ISBN 0-02-777460-0

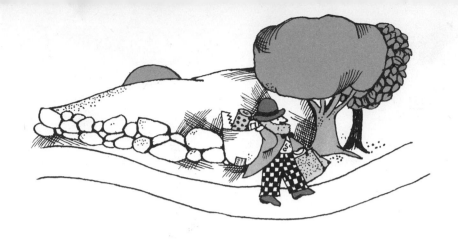

Chapter One

Timothy Todd came
down the road.
He said to himself,
"I will stop and see
Miller Moore.
I have a bag of sweet candy
for his son, Jack.
I will peddle the sweet candy
for a small bag of flour.

"Then I will stop
and see Widow Wilson.
I have some
pretty calico cloth
and I have some
needles and thread.
The calico cloth will make
pretty dresses
for Lizzy and Lucy.
I will peddle the calico cloth
for a fat pig.

"Then I will stop
and see Farmer Foote.
I have a good book
for Farmer Foote.
I will peddle the good book
for two big pumpkins.

"And then
maybe Farmer Foote
will let me spend the night
by his warm fire.
It is getting cold and dark,
so I must hurry."

Chapter Two

Timothy Todd came to
Miller Moore's mill.
"Hello," he said.
"Where is Jack?
I have some sweet candy
for him."

Miller Moore said,
"I do not know
where Jack is.
Maybe he is fishing.
Maybe he is climbing
a tree.
I will call him."
Miller Moore called Jack.
But Jack did not answer.
He called him
again and again.
But Jack did not answer.
"I will ask Mrs. Moore
where Jack is,"
said Miller Moore.

Mrs. Moore was working.
She was counting
bags of flour.
But she did not know
where Jack was.
"He will come home
for supper," she said.
Just then Timothy Todd
heard something.

"Tap! Tap! Tap!"
went something
at the window.
Timothy Todd looked.
So did Miller Moore
and Mrs. Moore.

Outside the window
they saw
three somethings.
They were white.
They were hiding
behind the bush.
They looked like
three big bags of flour.
One bag of flour moved.
One wiggled.

And one jumped up and said,
"Whooooo! Whoooooooo!"
Then they all ran away.

"Those are not bags of flour,"
  said Miller Moore.
"Those are ghosts.
  And I am scared of ghosts."
"Me too,"
  said Timothy Todd.
"And where is Jack?"
  said Mrs. Moore.
"Maybe those ghosts
  have stolen him."
  Mrs. Moore
  began to cry.
  Miller Moore did too.

Chapter Three

"Don't cry,"
   said Timothy Todd.
"I am scared of ghosts.
   That is true.
   But I have peddled
   on many lonely roads,
   and I have seen
   many strange things.

"I am a brave peddler.
I will find those ghosts.
I will tell them
to bring Jack home."
Mrs. Moore said,
"We will come too."

All three went
up the road.
Soon they came
to Loon Lake.
"Loooo! Loooo!"
called something.
"Ghosts!"
said Timothy Todd,
and he shivered.
"Shucks!"
said Miller Moore.
"That is not a ghost.
That is a loon.

"Ghosts say 'whooooo,'
and loons say 'looo.'
I am scared of ghosts.
But I am not scared
of loons."
And all three went on
up the road.

The moon came up.

An owl flew out of a tree.

"Hoot!" it said.

"That is not a ghost,"
  said Timothy Todd.
"That is an owl.
  Ghosts say 'whoooo,'
  and owls say 'hoot.'"
"Shhhh!" said Mrs. Moore.
"What is that?"
  They listened.

They heard something say,
"Whoooooooo!"
Then they heard it again.
They saw three white shapes
behind a tree.

"Those are not loons.
Those are not owls.
Those are ghosts!"
said Mrs. Moore.
"And those ghosts
have stolen Jack."
Mrs. Moore picked up a stick,
and she ran up the road.
Timothy Todd
and Miller Moore
ran up the road too.
But the ghosts ran faster.
They ran away.

Chapter Four

It was dark.
Far up the road
Timothy Todd saw
a little light.
It was not a house.
It was not a star.

The little light
came closer.
And it was not a ghost.
It was a lantern.
It was Widow Wilson's lantern.
She looked sad.

"Have you seen
   Lizzy and Lucy?"
   she said.
"It is time for supper.
   They have not peeled
   the potatoes.
   They have not set the table,
   and they have not
   brought in the wood.
   They have not come home,
   and I cannot find
   them anywhere."

"We have not seen
Lizzy and Lucy,"
said Miller Moore.
"And we cannot find Jack.
But we have seen
three ghosts.
We think they stole Jack.
Maybe they stole
Lizzy and Lucy too."

They heard something.
"Whooooooo! Whooooooo!"
The three ghosts
leaped out of the woods
and ran away.

Chapter Five

Timothy Todd ran
up the road.
So did Widow Wilson
and Miller Moore
and Mrs. Moore.

They were chasing
the ghosts.
"Oh, my," said Timothy Todd.
"Something is following us.
It is not three ghosts.
It is a bear
and a bobcat.
Maybe they are chasing
the three ghosts,
but maybe they are chasing us!"
Everyone ran faster.

They all ran past
Farmer Foote's cornfield.
They ran past his hayfield.
They saw the three ghosts
running around a haystack.
They ran through
Farmer Foote's pumpkin patch,
and the three ghosts did too.

When they came to
Farmer Foote's house,
his cow was mooing.
His chicken was clucking.
His goose was honking.
And his five fat pigs
were squealing.

Timothy Todd knocked
on Farmer Foote's door.
"Farmer Foote!
Farmer Foote!
Let us in! Let us in!
It is Timothy Todd,
and I have
a good book for you.
I also have Miller Moore
and Mrs. Moore
and Widow Wilson.

"Three ghosts
stole Jack
and Lizzy and Lucy.
We were chasing those ghosts.
But now
a bear and a bobcat
are chasing us!

Please open the door!

Please do!"

Farmer Foote opened the door.

"I do not want

bears and bobcats

in my house.

I do not want ghosts

in my house.

But you are my friends.

So come in quickly!"

And Farmer Foote

slammed the door.

"Shhhhh! What's that?"

said Timothy Todd.

Everyone listened.

"Whooooooooo!"
they heard,
and it was very loud.
"Those ghosts
are in this house!"
said Widow Wilson.
"They are behind that door,"
said Miller Moore.

"Oh, my!"
said Farmer Foote.
"I left my kitchen window open
so my cat could come home."
Farmer Foote
stamped his foot.
He started to cry.

"My cat did not come home,
but ghosts came in
my kitchen window.
I will go and hide."
"Me too,"
said Timothy Todd.

Mrs. Moore said,
"I will not hide.
I will make those ghosts
tell me where Jack is."

But just then

the door opened.

In came the three ghosts.

"Whooooooo!"

said the three ghosts.

"Where is Jack?"

said Mrs. Moore

and shook her stick.

"Where are Lizzy and Lucy?"

said Widow Wilson.

"We will tell you

where they are,"

said the biggest ghost

in a ghostly voice.

"We will tell you
    where they are
    if Timothy Todd will give us
    some good, sweet candy.
    Whooooooooo!"
"I have some good, sweet candy.
    That is true,"
    said Timothy Todd.
"I was saving it for Jack.
    But listen, ghosts,
    I will give it all to you
    if you will give back
    Jack and Lizzy and Lucy."

And Timothy Todd gave
the bag of candy
to the biggest ghost.

"Well, I never!"
said Mrs. Moore.
"Oh, shucks!"
said Timothy Todd.

Chapter Six

There were not three ghosts
any more.
There were Lizzy
and Lucy and Jack.
They were eating the candy.

Mrs. Moore hugged Jack.

Miller Moore did too.

Widow Wilson kissed
Lizzy and Lucy.

"Oh, my!" said Timothy Todd.

"I have been tricked
into giving them a treat."

"I am glad to see
all my friends tonight,"
said Farmer Foote.

"I was feeling lonesome.
I am so glad
to see you all. I think
we should have a party.

"I have some

big, juicy apples.

I have a pumpkin pie.

I will make some popcorn.

Then we can have a party."

And Farmer Foote went

into his kitchen.

"Help! Help!"

he shouted.

Everyone came running.

"Look!"

said Farmer Foote.

He pointed to his window.

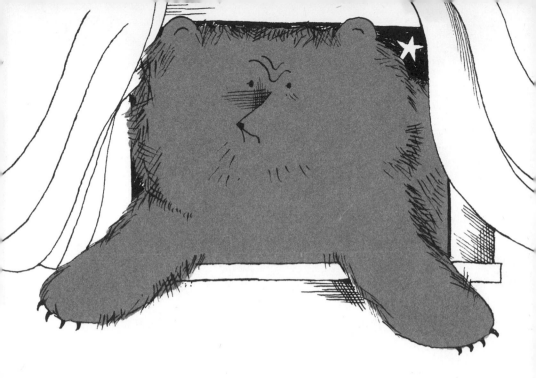

The bear was stuck
in the window.
"Umph," said the bear.
"He looks hungry,"
said Timothy Todd.
"I do not like hungry bears."
Lucy said,
"We will scare the bear away.
Wait and see."

Lizzy and Lucy and Jack
went out of the kitchen.
When they came back,
they were three ghosts.
"Whoooooooooo! Whooooooooo!"
they said
in ghostly voices.
The bear was scared.
He was so scared
he ran away.
The bobcat did too.

Farmer Foote carved
a scary face
on a big, fat pumpkin.
He put a candle
inside the pumpkin
and he lit the candle.

"Now no one will bother us,"
he said.
"Not bears.
Not bobcats.
Not ghosts."

And he popped the corn
and passed the apples
and gave everyone
a slice of pumpkin pie.